797,885 Books

are available to read at

Forgotten Books

www.ForgottenBooks.com

Forgotten Books' App
Available for mobile, tablet & eReader

ISBN 978-1-330-64613-7
PIBN 10086908

This book is a reproduction of an important historical work. Forgotten Books uses state-of-the-art technology to digitally reconstruct the work, preserving the original format whilst repairing imperfections present in the aged copy. In rare cases, an imperfection in the original, such as a blemish or missing page, may be replicated in our edition. We do, however, repair the vast majority of imperfections successfully; any imperfections that remain are intentionally left to preserve the state of such historical works.

Forgotten Books is a registered trademark of FB &c Ltd.
Copyright © 2017 FB &c Ltd.
FB &c Ltd, Dalton House, 60 Windsor Avenue, London, SW19 2RR.
Company number 08720141. Registered in England and Wales.

For support please visit www.forgottenbooks.com

1 MONTH OF FREE READING

at

www.ForgottenBooks.com

By purchasing this book you are eligible for one month membership to ForgottenBooks.com, giving you unlimited access to our entire collection of over 700,000 titles via our web site and mobile apps.

To claim your free month visit: www.forgottenbooks.com/free86908

* Offer is valid for 45 days from date of purchase. Terms and conditions apply.

English
Français
Deutsche
Italiano
Español
Português

www.forgottenbooks.com

Mythology Photography **Fiction**
Fishing Christianity **Art** Cooking
Essays Buddhism Freemasonry
Medicine **Biology** Music **Ancient Egypt** Evolution Carpentry Physics
Dance Geology **Mathematics** Fitness
Shakespeare **Folklore** Yoga Marketing
Confidence Immortality Biographies
Poetry **Psychology** Witchcraft
Electronics Chemistry History **Law**
Accounting **Philosophy** Anthropology
Alchemy Drama Quantum Mechanics
Atheism Sexual Health **Ancient History**
Entrepreneurship Languages Sport
Paleontology Needlework Islam
Metaphysics Investment Archaeology
Parenting Statistics Criminology
Motivational

THE "OCTAVIUS" OF MINUCIUS

FREELY TRANSLATED BY
ARTHUR AIKIN BRODRIBB

GEORGE BELL & SONS
1903

CHISWICK PRESS : CHARLES WHITTINGHAM AND CO.
TOOKS COURT, CHANCERY LANE, LONDON.

INTRODUCTION

THE "Octavius," the only known work of Marcus Minucius Felix, contains two speeches on religion, one from the Pagan, and the other from the Christian point of view. Short as it is, this almost classical dialogue holds an important place in literature as the earliest extant defence of Christianity by a Latin writer; that is, if, as there is reason to believe, Minucius is prior to Tertullian. But, whether prior to Tertullian or not, he was highly esteemed in his own time, and by subsequent writers, one of whom, Cyprian, published a treatise on "Idols," which is so absolutely plagiarized from the "Octavius" that the text of Cyprian occasionally serves to elucidate that of Minucius.

Minucius, however, was unknown during a great part of the middle ages. The only manuscript of the "Octavius" is a minuscule of the ninth century, and has been for many years in the Paris library. It is headed: "Arnobii liber VII explicit. Incipit liber VIII feliciter." Now, Arnobius's celebrated work against the Pagans contains only seven books; there is no eighth book of Arnobius. Unfortunately, when these seven books were first edited and printed, at Rome in 1543, this manuscript of the "Octavius" was associated with them, and was printed with them as a Liber Octavus; a mistake which was repeated in the two succeeding editions. François Baudouin, or Balduinus, in his Heidelberg edition of 1560, was the first to publish the supposed Liber Octavus of Arnobius as the "Octavius" of Minucius. His edition contains a long Latin dissertation, in which he claims the work for its real author and expresses his surprise that the mistake should have escaped the notice of so great a scholar as Erasmus.

Since 1560 Minucius has received much attention from scholars, but the text, after continual revision and emendation, still offers a great many doubtful readings.

There is no external evidence for so much as a single fact in the life of Minucius. All that is known, or is supposed to be known, of him is derived from the introduction to his book. From this we gather that he was a convert to Christianity, a lawyer, and by residence, if not by birth, a Roman. But this is all, and if we hold that the introduction, which certainly resembles a work of art, is only a contrivance for bringing together imaginary opponents for an imaginary debate, we shall have to own that we know nothing of Minucius except his name. That, however, is not the view taken by the best authorities. They do not regard the introduction as fictitious, and their opinion is corroborated by inscriptions found at Cirta in Africa, which show that one of the speakers, who is described by Minucius as a compatriot of the orator Fronto of Cirta, was, in fact, a native of that place. We may take it, then, that the introduction gives a true account, as far as it goes, of Minucius himself. The speeches, it need hardly be said, owe their literary form to the author, who must have heard many similar arguments in the course of his life.

We do not know in what years Minucius was born and died, and the date of his work has been the subject of much controversy. The statements of Lactantius and Jerome do not help us. Apparently, the question is rendered insoluble by the peculiar nature of the book itself. Minucius writes his recollection of a formal argument between two of his friends, one of whom is described as dead at the time of writing, while the other is, presumably, still alive. Internal evidence points to the year 162 or 163 as the probable date of the argument. But the date of the argument, whatever it may be, cannot be the date of the book, which the author expressly declares to be written from memory, he does not say how many years later, after his friend's death. The interval that separates these two dates must therefore remain uncertain. Perhaps it will be enough to say that most modern critics place Minucius in the second and not in the third century.

In the extremely graceful introduction the three friends, Marcus Minucius Felix, Octavius Januarius and Quintus Caecilius Natalis, take a morning walk on the sands at Ostia, a seaside place at the mouth of the Tiber, not far from Rome. Minucius and Octavius are Christians; Caecilius adheres to the old religion. At the beginning of the walk, Octavius makes a casual remark which sounds like a challenge to Caecilius to defend his views. Later on, the subject is referred to again, and is then debated, Minucius remaining neutral, and acting as judge. Caecilius at length owns that he has been induced to change his opinions.

The argument of Caecilius may be thus summarized: "Our knowledge of the universe is necessarily limited, but we have no reason, on any hypothesis, to postulate divine agency. The available evidence suggests that chance prevails rather than providence, but, as the fact cannot be established, our ancestral faith is safer and better than vague speculations. And see how much Rome owes to her ancestral faith, and how invincible it has made her. It is true that we do not know the nature of the gods; but they cannot be ignored, and all history shows that it is prudent to pay attention to their omens. The Christians, certainly, are not entitled to attack them, and they do not seem to have anything better to offer. They belong to the lowest and most ignorant classes, their immorality is notorious, they worship a criminal and his cross, they reverence the head of an ass, they practice the ritual murder of infants, their meetings are nocturnal and secret, their feasts are impure,

INTRODUCTION

their lives are miserable and colourless, and they hold absurd notions as to the end of the world, a resurrection of the dead, and an omniscient and omnipresent God. Such are the people who presume to pronounce an opinion on subjects as to which philosophers have wisely maintained an attitude of reserve."

Octavius replies: "Your expressions are harsh, and I am not sure whether you do or do not believe in the effective existence of your gods. Ignorant as we may be, man's place in nature compels him to an inquiry into the universe and the attributes of its Governor. For, unquestionably, it has a Governor, whose handiwork it is, and is ruled, not by chance but by Providence. Polytheism is untenable, and has not the support of philosophers, all of whom regard God as some phase of intangible Unity. On the other hand, your own gods, such as Saturn and Jupiter, are only legendary human beings who were deified in an age of credulity. Their rites are undignified, and often shocking. Can you seriously maintain that the Roman power owes anything to their patronage? As to omens and oracles, it is a fallacy to connect them with victory or defeat. The truth is that they are controlled by daemons, fallen spirits, who actuate the whole machinery of your religion, and do their utmost to excite prejudice against us. How stale your charges against us are! And how is it that none of them have ever been proved? You say that we worship the head of an ass; that we render divine honours to a crucified criminal; that we murder children; that our meetings are scenes of debauchery. Nothing of the sort. These are imputations the like of which, in an aggravated form, might be retorted against your own impure superstitions. You think that we have some mysterious concealed object of worship. We worship God; how can God be concealed anywhere? You think our doctrines nonsense. The germs of them are to be found in your own philosophers. No; you are doing us a great injustice; you do not understand that, though most of us are poor, we are also sober, clean-living, hopeful, and happy; happy even under persecution and torture. I care nothing for your cautious philosophers who boast of their attitude of reserve. Let them debate away, by all means, as long as ever they like. I am only thankful that God has made us more enlightened."

These speeches are of course the work of

Minucius. He has arranged them for publication, and has made them literature; but there is no reason to doubt his statement that they represent the arguments actually used by his friends. From the speech of Caecilius, who is apparently a young lawyer, we may gather the religious views of the average educated Roman. He is called upon, not quite on the spur of the moment, to defend his belief, and, having had time to collect his thoughts, he states his case in an orderly way, at least as well as most young men would have stated it. He knows something of history and philosophy, and, though he is not well-informed about the Christians, one or two of their doctrines are known to him, and he is familiar with all that was commonly reported to their discredit. Like other Romans, he feels sure that when ignorant and eccentric people meet in private their proceedings will not bear investigation. Minucius takes care that he shall repeat all the usual slanders against the Christians, for these he intends to answer fully in the speech of Octavius.

The much longer reply of Octavius, full of learning derived from earlier writers, and especially from Cicero, traverses almost every word that has been uttered by Caecilius. In this respect it is so systematic and precise as to be evidently the work, not of a theologian, but of a lawyer. Caecilius leans to the doctrine of chance, believes in a plurality of gods, and despises the Christians. Octavius substitutes providence for chance, one God for many gods, and vindicates the character of the Christian community. Except for the curious passage on daemons, he does not once travel beyond his brief, but contents himself with an argument strictly limited by that of his opponent. But the lawyer is also a literary artist. He puts into the mouth of Octavius a reply that is complete and sufficient for his purpose, and does not concern himself with what has not been advanced, or with doctrines that Caecilius cannot immediately discuss or accept. His object is simply the refutation of Caecilius; to attempt more would spoil the artistic design of the work, and would render it imperfect, introductory, and open to further challenge. The reticence of Minucius, and the fact that he has little or nothing to say of the cardinal doctrines of Christianity, have often been remarked, and it has even been suggested that he was himself not so much a Christian as a Theist. But the explanation is that he is not as yet instructing a convert, but is only endeavouring to make one. For the present he is appealing, not altogether on Christian grounds but rather on general grounds, to a hostile audience. And the hostile audience, whose philosophers and poets and historians he summons as witnesses on his own side, though it consists nominally of Caecilius alone, comprises in reality all Rome, where at this time hardly one man in twenty was a Christian. If he can remove prejudice, and show that the new religion is, on the face of it, more rational than the old, he may obtain a hearing. That, and for the present nothing more, seems to be the purpose of the work.

For the following free translation the editions of Baehrens, 1886, and of Waltzing, 1903, have been used. They differ in many places; but a free rendering may perhaps adopt the reading sometimes of the one, and sometimes of the other. The state of the text is such that finality cannot be claimed for any particular edition. The places in which important emendations by Baehrens have been followed are indicated in the notes.

OCTAVIUS

WHENEVER my thoughts dwell on my good old friend Octavius, his charming and lovable personality becomes so real to me that I seem in a manner to return to the past, with something more than a mere recollection of its closed pages. My eyes can no longer see him, but his portrait is for that very reason all the more deeply engraved on my heart and my inmost feelings. He was a remarkable and saintly man, and his departure from this world left me with an indefinite sense of loss. In truth, he was so much attached to me that our thoughts and wishes, whether grave or gay, always coincided; it was as though we had only one mind between us. The result of this unanimity was that, while he was the only partner of my pleasures, he shared my errors also. So, again, when I escaped from the dark slough of ignorance into the light of wisdom and truth, he did not cast off his companion, but, much more nobly, ran on to show him the way. Consequently, when my thoughts range over the whole period of our intimacy, my most vivid recollection is of a discourse of his in which by sheer force of argument he converted Quintus Caecilius from his belated superstition to the true faith.

Octavius had come to Rome partly on business, and partly in order to see me; and he had left his wife and children at home, the little ones just at the age of innocence, and at that most lovable time when they try to say short words with delightfully quaint attempts at pronunciation. I cannot say how pleased I was to see my greatest friend, especially as his arrival was quite unexpected. After a day or two of renewed intimacy, when we had to some extent satisfied our hunger for each other's company, and had thoroughly compared notes together, we determined to go to Ostia, an exceedingly nice place, where I had been advised to try the bracing effects of sea-bathing. The vintage holidays had released me from the law-courts, and after the heat of summer there was a touch of autumn in the air.

OCTAVIUS

Well, early one morning we were walking down to the sea, to enjoy the cool breeze and a stroll over the sands, when Caecilius, who was with us, noticed an image of Serapis,[1] and in the usual superstitious way kissed his hand to it.

Then Octavius said to me: "Marcus, my brother, here is a man who is closely connected with you, both in private life and in business. You are not doing your duty by him if you leave him in ignorant blindness, and let him stumble in broad daylight over blocks of stone, even though they are carved and anointed and crowned. You must be aware that his error is as discreditable to yourself as it is to him."

This remark brought us past the town to the open shore, where the gentle waves had made us a promenade of level sand. The sea, which is never absolutely still, even when there is no wind, came in, not white and foaming, but in curling, twisting waves which it was a pleasure to look at, and, when we walked quite at the edge of the water, played round our footsteps and then receded from

[1] See note at end.

them. So we walked on, slowly and quietly, along the slight curve of the shore, amusing ourselves with conversation and with Octavius's accounts of his experiences on board ship. When we had gone far enough, walking and talking, we turned to come back the same way, and, as we came to a place where some boats were laid up high and dry upon baulks of timber, we saw a number of boys playing at ducks and drakes with bits of tile. The game, of course, is to choose a flat piece, with rounded edges, and then, holding it low, to throw it so that it may skim the surface of the water and make as many hops and jumps as possible; and the boy whose shot goes farthest and jumps oftenest is the winner.

The sight distinctly amused Octavius and me, but Caecilius took no notice of it and did not so much as smile, but showed by his preoccupied expression that he was trying to keep to himself something or other that had annoyed him.

"Now, Caecilius," said I, "what is the matter with you? What has become of all your gaiety? You generally look more cheerful than that even on serious occasions."

"It is that nasty remark of our friend

Octavius," he replied, "that has been irritating me all this time. It was addressed ostensibly to you, because he blamed your negligence; but that was only his indirect way of charging me with ignorance, which is worse. As he has practically raised the whole question, the matter cannot rest where it is, so I shall have to have it out with him. All I know is that, if he wants me to argue on behalf of the school I belong to, he will soon find it easier to wrangle among his friends than to conduct a philosophical discussion. However, suppose we sit down on this stone breakwater by the baths, and rest, and thresh it out."

So we sat down as he suggested, with myself in the middle; not that etiquette demanded that I should have the place of honour, because friendship always assumes or makes equality, but in order that I might act as judge, and hear both sides equally, and part the combatants.

Then Caecilius began:

"I know that you, brother Marcus, have made up your mind on the main subject of our discussion, and that, after honestly trying both ways of life, you have rejected the one and have chosen the other. All the same, your mental attitude for the present must be that of a judge who holds the scales evenly, and you must not lean to either side, or your judgement will seem to result less from our arguments than from your own sympathies. Remember, you are sitting judicially, as a stranger to both parties. Now, that being so, it ought not to be difficult for me to show that all our human speculations are doubtful and provisional; plausible, it may be, but not verified. That makes it all the more surprising that, when people get tired of investigation, so many of them should fall easy victims to almost any theory rather than persevere doggedly in the inquiry. But when uncultivated and illiterate persons, without even a skilled workman's training, pronounce confidently on the highest and most abstract questions which all schools of philosophy in all ages have debated and are still debating, I suppose that everyone must condemn and regret their presumption. And rightly, for our human limitations render us quite unequal to these theological inquiries. We do not know, and we may not examine, and we cannot without irreverence theorize about what is high above us in the heavens or is buried far below us in the earth.

"Truly, we may think ourselves happy enough, and wise enough, if we take the advice of the old sage, and cultivate a better knowledge of ourselves. However, we are so attracted by the foolish ambition to exceed our limited capacities that, while we grovel on earth, we aspire to penetrate to heaven itself and the very stars. Yet even so we need not aggravate our blunder by wild and dreadful imaginings. Suppose, as the origin of everything, a natural concourse of atoms; why postulate divine agency? Or suppose that a fortuitous concourse of atoms formed and consolidated the various parts of the universe; why introduce a divine artificer? Or say simply that fire kindled the stars, that the heavens float because they are light, that the earth is fixed because it is heavy, and that the sea is an accumulation of water; how do religion, dread of God, and superstition enter into that statement of the case? The fact is that man and every animal that is born and lives and grows, is a spontaneous concretion of elements into which he, with every living thing, is ultimately resolved. All things return to their source in automatic revolution, without any external interference or agency. In this way, when particles of fire are collected, new suns are continually formed; when vapours are exhaled from the land, they become mists; when these thicken and are driven together, they form banks of clouds, and, when these fall, down come rain and squalls and hail, or, if the storm-clouds meet, thunder and lightning and thunder-bolts. And observe, these fall everywhere; they attack the mountains and the trees; they affect all places indiscriminately, whether holy or profane, and strike all men, whether saints or sinners. I need not remind you of the uncertainty and caprice of storms, in which all nature seems to be involved without rule or reason; or of shipwrecks, where good and bad meet a common fate without regard to their deserts; or of fires, in which the guilty and the innocent are alike consumed. In an epidemic, are not all carried off without distinction? In battle, do not the best men generally fall? In peace, on the other hand, wickedness is not only put on an equality with virtue, but is so favoured that in a good many cases one envies the prosperity of the criminal as much as one detests his crimes. No; if the world were governed by divine providence, and were under the supreme authority of any one deity, divine justice would never have awarded thrones to Phalaris and Dionysius, exile to Rutilius and Camillus, and poison to Socrates. Look at the loaded fruit-trees, the ripe cornfields, the juicy vineyards; look at them, and see them ruined by rain, or beaten down by hail. The fact is, either the destined event is hidden and concealed from us, or, as is more probable, lawless chance, with its endless critical contingencies, rules everything.

"But in either case, with destiny so uncertain, and nature so capricious, how much better and more reverent it is for us to take the teaching of our ancestors as the witness of the truth; to keep our traditional religion, to worship the gods whom our parents taught us to fear before knowing them familiarly, and, instead of dogmatizing on theology, to follow our forefathers who, in the first rough ages of the world, rightly esteemed their gods as either servants or kings. That is the reason why every state, province and town has its own sacred rites, and worships its local civic gods. The Eleusinians worship Ceres, the Phrygians

Cybele, the Epidaurians Aesculapius, the Chaldaeans Belus, the Syrians Astarte, the Taurians Diana, the Gauls Mercury, the Romans all of them. The Romans have filled the whole world with their power and authority, and have extended their rule beyond the paths of the sun and the bounds of ocean. And why? Because with them religion and valour go hand in hand; because the strength of their city is in the sanctity of religious rites, pure priestesses, and priests of many degrees and titles; because, when the city was besieged and taken, all but the Capitol, they remained true to the gods whom others would have cast off in anger, and, while the Gauls wondered at their confident faith, marched through their ranks with no other arms than religious devotion; because, when they take a city, they honour the gods of their beaten foes even in the first flush of victory; because everywhere they seek to make the gods their guests and their own; because they sometimes build altars to unknown gods and spirits. Thus they have adopted the religion, and have earned the dominions, of all nations. And thus the uninterrupted continuance of our religion has endured, not weakened, but fortified by the lapse of ages; and the holiness of our ceremonies and temples has increased with their lengthening antiquity.

"Still, for I may venture to make the concession, and in doing so to err on the safe side, our ancestors were well advised in consulting auguries, observing omens, instituting ceremonies, and dedicating shrines. If you look at the record of history, you will find that all religious rites originated in the desire to recompense the gods for their favour, or to avert coming wrath, or to mitigate its threatening violence. I may instance the worship of the Idaean mother, whose coming proved the virtue of a matron and saved the city from the fear of the enemy; the sacred statues of the twin horsemen by the lake, as they appeared, breathless on foaming and smoking steeds, and announced the victory they had won that very day over Perseus; the renewal, in consequence of a countryfellow's dream, of the games in honour of the offended Jupiter; the determined devotion of the Decii; and Curtius, who closed up a yawning chasm by plunging into it on horseback. Only too often has the neglect of auspices attested the power of the gods. For this reason, Allia is a name of evil omen; and the wreck of the fleet of Claudius and Junius, if not their battle with the Carthaginians, is a mournful memory. Flaminius contemned the auguries, and Trasymenus was swollen and reddened with Roman blood; and Crassus laughed at, and deserved, the imprecations of the Furies with the result that we are still recovering our standards from the Parthians.[2] I say nothing of a number of old stories, I ignore what the poets have said about the birthdays of the gods, and their gifts and presents; I even pass over instances of fate foretold by oracles, lest you should think ancient history too fabulous. But consider the temples and shrines of the gods, which protect and adorn the Roman state; it is no wealth of decoration, of gifts and offerings, that makes them glorious, but the indwelling, the presence, the tenancy of the gods themselves. There divinely inspired priests dip into the future, give counsel in danger, medicine in sickness, hope to the afflicted, help to the desolate, comfort in calamity, and relief in distress. Deny them, reject them, forswear them as we may in the daytime, in the quiet of night we see and hear and recognize the gods.

"And therefore, as there is a substantial agreement among all nations as to the immortal gods, whatever the explanation and origin of them may be, it is intolerable that any-one should be so puffed up with audacity and profane conceit as to endeavour to destroy or weaken so old, so useful, so wholesome a religion. There were, of course, Theodorus of Cyrene, and his predecessor Diagoras of Melos, who was formerly surnamed the Atheist. They declared that there were no gods, and did their best to abolish the fear and sense of religion by which the human race is influenced. But these sham philosophies, with their blasphemous tenets, will never have any formidable following or authority. Considering that when Protagoras of Abdera was arguing about the nature of the gods, not profanely, but only rationally, the Athenians banished him and publicly burned his writings, well—you must excuse my vehemence—but is it not lamentable that members of an unlawful and hopelessly discredited sect should assail the gods? These are the people who get together the lowest and most ignorant classes, and foolish women with all the gullibility of their sex, and start a profane society of conspirators which meets at night and is bound together by solemn fasts and inhuman food, and not by any holy rite, but by a crime. It is a tribe that loves hiding-places and darkness, says nothing in public, but is talkative enough in secret corners. They despise the temples as mere burial places, spit at the gods, and jeer at holy things. They pity our priests in spite of their own pitiable condition, and look down upon appointments and robes of office, though they are themselves almost in rags. What amazing folly; what incredible impudence! They think nothing of present torture, but dread what is uncertain and future; and they fear death after death, but are not afraid to die in the meantime, the fact being that an illusory hope soothes their terrors and consoles them with the prospect of another life.

Ill weeds grow apace, and already, with the daily increase of immorality, there is everywhere an increase of these disgusting and profane meetings. The conspiracy must be cut out[3] and utterly uprooted. They recognize each other by private marks and signs; they profess to love one another before they are actually acquainted; everywhere among them there is a quasi-religious strain of grossness, and they call each other 'brother' and 'sister' promiscuously in order that these hallowed names may give zest to ordinary sin. Thus their vain and insane superstition glories in crime. Nor would rumour, well informed as it is, say the most atrocious unmentionable things of them without a substratum of truth. I hear that they consecrate and worship—I know not with what absurd idea—the head of an ass,[4] the most abject of all creatures. Their religion is indeed appropriate to the customs in which it originates! Others speak of a still less decorous object of their veneration.[5] This may not be true, but suspicion inevitably attaches to secret and nocturnal ceremonies. And the story that they accord a religious sanctity to a man who was put to death for his crime, and to the wood of the fatal cross, provides very suitable holy things for these wretches, and enables them to worship what they deserve. As for their method of initiating neophytes, the account is as horrible as it is notorious. A baby is completely hidden under a quantity of meal, and is placed before the person who is to be initiated. The unwary novice is directed to stab into what looks like a mass of meal, and in doing so unintentionally kills the child. Then—how shocking it all is—they greedily lap up the child's blood, and sever his limbs. This is the sacrifice that binds them together; this is the guilty secret that pledges them all mutually to silence. Rites like these are worse than the worst sacrilege. We know, too, about their feasts; it is common talk, and is borne out by the speech of my fellow-countryman, Fronto of Cirta.[6] They meet for their feast on an appointed day, with all their wives, children, sisters and mothers; people of both sexes and all ages, and then, after a full meal, when everyone has become excited—but why describe such a scene of debauchery?[7]

"I pass over many other things deliberately. These are more than enough, and the mere secresy of this corrupt religion proclaims the truth of all, or almost all, of them. Now, why do they take such great pains to conceal what they worship? Honesty loves the light of day; crime hides its head. Why have they no altars, no temples, no famous images, no public addresses, no open meetings, if what they worship so mysteriously is neither illegal nor shameful? And whence, and who, and where is this one solitary lonely God of theirs who is unknown to every free people and kingdom, and even to Roman superstition? The unique and miserable Jewish race had one God, but they worshipped him openly, with temples, altars, sacrifices, and ceremonies; and he had so little power and influence that he and his own peculiar nation have been captured by mere mortal Romans. But the Christians, what portentous monsters they invent! They pretend that this God of theirs, whom they can neither show nor see, diligently scrutinizes the hearts of all, the acts of all, and even words and secret thoughts, in his ubiquitous ramblings. Their conception is of a troublesome and restless deity, who is at once ineffective[3] and inquisitive, because, if he is a party to all that goes on, and roams about everywhere, his universal cares would make him useless to individuals, while his attention to individuals would preclude his universal utility.

"Then again, what is to be said for their doctrine that the world itself, and the universe with its stars will some day be burnt up and ruined? As if the eternal order of nature, settled by divine laws, could be disturbed; as if the elements could break their bonds, and the heavenly framework split, and the vast mass in which everything is contained be overthrown! And not content with this absurdity, they tack on to it a parcel of tales fit only for old women. They say that, after death and dust and ashes, they are born again; and they encourage each other to believe their lies with such unaccountable confidence that you would imagine that they had already found them true. These delusions involve the doubly lunatic prophecy of destruction to the heavens and the stars, which we leave exactly as we found them, and of eternity, when we are dead and done with, to ourselves, who die as naturally as we are born. For that reason, I believe, they denounce cremation; as if every corpse, whether burnt or not, was not sooner or later resolved into earth; as if it mattered whether wild beasts tore it in pieces, or the sea swallowed it up, or the ground covered it, or fire consumed it. If corpses feel, every way of disposing of them must be painful; if they do not, cremation, as the speediest mode, must be a benefit. With these mistaken ideas they deceive themselves, and look forward to a life of endless happiness after death; while to the rest, that is, the wicked, they assign eternal punishment. On this I might say much, only my argument must hasten on. I need not labour the point that they are morally bad, for by this time I have proved it. And yet, if I pronounced in their favour, I should have to bear in mind the general opinion that both badness and goodness are attributable to fate; and this must also be your own view, because, while we ascribe all human action to fate, you ascribe it to God, and people join your sect, not spontaneously, but when they are called. Your hypothesis, then, is of an unjust judge, who punishes men not for their will, but for their circumstances.

"But as regards this future life, I should like to know, is this resurrection to be without, or with, our bodies; and with what bodies; with our old bodies, or with new ones? Without the body? That, as far as I can see, it neither mind, nor soul, nor life. With the same body? Well, but it has already perished. With another body? In that case it is new birth, not restored existence. And really, in the whole course of time, after all these innumerable ages, is there a single authentic instance of any person's return from the lower regions, even with the short three hours' leave of absence granted to Protesilaus? All these figments of a diseased imagination, all these purely ornamental poetical legends you have unblushingly furbished up in order to support your too[9] credulous belief in your God.

"And yet you do not perceive from your present circumstances how you are deceived by false hopes and empty promises. You poor people, learn while you are alive what you may expect after death. Look at the greater part of your people—the 'better' part, as you call them—and see how they suffer from want, cold, drudgery and hunger. And God allows it all, and pretends that it is nothing, and is either so powerless or so unjust that he will not, or cannot, help his own! You, who dream of posthumous immortality, when you are unnerved by danger, parched by fever, or racked with pain, are you still unconscious of your own condition? Do you not recognize your weakness? My poor fellow, you are convicted, in spite of yourself, of an infirmity that you will not acknowledge. But these are commonplaces, and I pass on. See what is in store for you, pains and penalties and tortures; and crosses, not to be adored but endured; and fires, too, such as you predict and fear. And where is that God who can help you when you come to life again, but not while you are alive? Do not the Romans rule without any help from your God? Of course they do; they enjoy the whole world, and they are your masters. But as for you, you walk in fear and trembling, you abstain from honest pleasures, you never go to the theatres, you take no part in public processions and feasts, you loathe the sacred contests, and you abhor meat and drink that has been taken from our altars. Apparently, you are afraid of the gods whom you deny. You wear no flowers in your hair, and you use no sweet-smelling unguents, but keep them for funerals. You even refuse wreaths of flowers for your graves. Truly, a cheerless, pale-faced set of people, who deserve all pity, even from our own gods; for you are in this unfortunate position, that you neither rise again nor live while you may. If you have any sense or modesty, you will pry no more into the regions of heaven and into the hidden destinies of the world. It is enough for very ignorant and uncultivated people to see what is at their feet. When men cannot understand human affairs, assuredly they must not be allowed to argue about divinity.

"Still, if you positively must philosophize, let any one of your sect who is equal to it imitate, if he can, Socrates, the very prince of wisdom. Whenever he was asked about heavenly things, he gave the famous answer, 'that which is above us is nothing to us.' He well deserved the oracle's testimony to his singular wisdom, and, indeed, suspected what it was that raised him above other men; not that he had discovered everything, but because he had learned that he knew nothing. In this way the confession of ignorance is a very high form of wisdom. From this principle came the unassailable scepticism of Arcesilaus and, a good deal later, of Carneades and most of the Academics on all the most abstruse speculations; and this is the kind of philosophy in which the unlearned may indulge cautiously and the learned with confidence. Surely, we must all admire and try to follow the deliberation of Simonides, the lyric poet. When King Hiero asked Simonides what he thought the gods were, and of what nature, he took a day to consider the question, and on the morrow asked for two days more, and then demanded another. And finally, when the king asked the reason for so much delay, he answered that the more he reflected on the subject the more obscure he found it. That is my own opinion too. When things are doubtful, it is best to leave them alone; and, when so many great men have debated them, you must not come, hastily and presumptuously, to any definite conclusion. Otherwise, the result will be, either some foolish superstition, or the destruction of all religion."

Such was the speech of Caecilius. His indignation had subsided in the flow of his oratory, and he said with a smile:

"What answer to all this shall we have from our aggressive friend, Octavius, a most eminent man among nobodies, but the last and least of philosophers?"[10]

"Wait a little before you crow over him," said I; "your rejoicings will be out of order until both sides have been heard, especially as the object of your discussion is not a personal triumph, but truth. And I must say that, though I was much pleased with your ingenious and varied argument, what impresses me most, not in this particular discussion, but in all controversy, is the way in which even obvious truths are affected by the ability and the eloquence of the speaker. Very often his hearers are too sympathetic. Words fascinate them so much that they are apt to lose their grip of ideas and assent casually to all sorts of propositions, with no real perception of truth and error, and no appreciation of the fact that the incredible may be more or less true, and the probable more or less false. Whatever they assent to, some clever person is sure to prove them in the wrong; and the result is that, after being repeatedly misled by their own hasty conclusions, they fancy that what bewilders them is the inherent uncertainty of the question. Ultimately, with a fine condemnation of dogma, they avoid the risk of error by expressing no opinions at all. This being so, let us try to avoid everything that has brought controversy into disrepute, and has led simple-minded people to detest it. We must remember that some people are easy-going and credulous, and that, when they are misled by their trusted guides, they naturally suspect everybody and fear the evil designs of their best friends. In a controversy that is hard-fought on both sides, truth is often obscure, and, thanks to eloquence, sheer subtleties are often made to look like first principles. I am particularly anxious, then, to weigh every argument carefully, so that, while recognizing ingenuity, we may find out and determine the truth."

"You are departing," said Caecilius, "from the duty of an impartial judge, for it is very unfair that you should blunt the edge of my argument by interpolating these important considerations. Octavius has to answer my case, if he can, and he ought to have it before him fresh and untouched."

"I did what you object to," I rejoined, "for our mutual advantage, as I thought; and my object was that the scales of justice should be made to respond, not to frothy rhetoric, but to the solid merits of the case. However, there shall be no further digression, since you dislike it. Let us listen quietly to the reply which our friend Octavius is burning to make."

Then Octavius said: "I will reply to the best of my ability, and we must use our joint endeavours to wash away the stain of Caecilius's bitter reproaches in the waters of truth. I must honestly say, at the outset, that our friend's opinions are so vague and indefinite as to raise a doubt in my mind whether the confusion was intentional or was the result of real misconception. He said at one moment that he believed in the gods, and at another that he was making up his mind about them. It looked as if his object was to make the basis of my reply even more shifting and more doubtful than his own position. But really, I hesitate to charge our friend with anything so disingenuous. I feel sure that sharp practice is foreign to his honest nature. But how am I to account for it? When a man does not know his way, and comes to a place where the road branches off into several roads, he is pulled up uncomfortably, not venturing to take any one of them, and not able to try them all. So it is when a man has no settled convictions; his ideas are at the mercy of every shallow doubt that presents itself. It seems to me quite natural that the eddies and cross-currents of opinion should drive Caecilius into contrarieties and inconsistencies. However, this need not happen to him again. I shall be able to refute his arguments, notwithstanding their diversity, by establishing the truth, and nothing but the truth; and then he ought not to doubt or lose his way any more.

"Our friend expressed a good deal of anger and disgust and indignation at the thought of poor and uneducated persons discussing divine things. I would have him know, however, that all human beings, no matter of what age or sex or rank, are endowed at birth with the faculty of reason and sense, and that men have acquired wisdom by their natural ability, and not by virtue of their station in life. Even the philosophers themselves, and those pioneers of civilization whose names have come down to us, were regarded as ignorant and shabby plebeians until their intellectual eminence was recognized. While the rich, engrossed in their wealth, habitually thought more of money than of the heavens, poverty-stricken [11] thinkers made great discoveries, and handed down the tradition of learning. Evidently, brains cannot be purchased either by love or money, but are born with us as part and parcel of our intellectual equipment. You need not, therefore, be in the least aggrieved or indignant that any one, be he who he may, should inquire into divine things, and form and express an opinion upon them. What is important is, not the qualification of the arguer, but the truth of the argument. Indeed, the simpler the discourse, the brighter its light, since it is not coloured by any show of eloquence and grace, but is sustained on its own merits by its directness and honesty.

"I do not deny one of Caecilius's main contentions, that man ought to know himself, and look round and consider what he is, whence he comes, and why he is here; and whether he is a concretion of elements or a harmonizing of atoms, or whether it is not more likely that his body and soul are the work of God. But this involves an inquiry into the universe, for all these questions are so closely connected that, until you have thoroughly investigated the philosophy of God, you cannot know that of man; just as you cannot excel in human politics without a knowledge of the world of which we are all of us citizens. And inquire we must, if only because man differs from wild beasts. These look downwards, intent on the earth, and food is the limit of their natural horizon. But we, with our uplifted face, our gaze into heaven, our mind, and our reason with which we recognize and feel and imitate God, we cannot, we must not ignore the celestial brightness which forces itself upon our eyes and our senses. It would be most irreverent to search below for that which you ought to find on high. In my opinion, those who hold that all this well-ordered cosmic system has not been perfected by divine reason, but is only a conglomeration of casually cohering fragments, are literally as well as metaphorically blind. When you look up to heaven and then turn your eyes to all that is below it and around you, what can be plainer and more obvious than that there must be some supremely intelligent power by which all nature is inspired, moved, sustained, and directed? Look at the heaven itself, and see how far it stretches and how fast it revolves, both when it is hung with stars by night and when the sun lights it by day; you cannot but regard it as the marvellous and divinely balanced work of a consummate author. See how the year results from the circuit of the sun, and the month from the waxing and waning of the moon. Notice also the alternation of light and darkness, which permits us our own alternation of work and rest. I must leave to astronomers the more complete consideration of the stars as our guides in navigation, and as determining the seasons of ploughing and harvest. The mere phenomena cannot be observed and understood without much scientific knowledge, but for the actual creation and ordering of each star a supreme artificer and perfect intelligence are demanded. And I put it to you, if seasons and crops always follow one another in the same orderly succession, do not flowers in spring, harvest in summer, fruit in autumn, and the indispensable olive in winter all equally proclaim their great original, their parent? All in due sequence; yet the due sequence might easily fail if it were not ordered by the highest wisdom. Again, how well providence is shown in the mild weather of autumn and spring, which intervenes to prevent us from being frozen or scorched by the extremes of winter cold and summer heat, and so renders the passage of the returning year imperceptible and harmless! Look at every tree, how it is nourished out of the lap of earth; notice the streams with their perennial springs; and the rivers, always gliding onwards; look at the sea, how it is bound within its limits; and the ocean, with its flowing and ebbing tides. Why speak of conveniently placed ranges of mountains, slopes of hills, and stretches of plain? Why speak of the manifold ways in which animals protect themselves, some with horns, some with teeth, some with claws, and some with stings, while others escape danger by their speed, or their wings? But most of all, the beauty of the human form confesses its divine maker; the erect posture, the upward countenance, the eyes high in the summit of the body as in a watch-tower, and all the other senses concentrated like a garrison in a citadel.

"It would take me too long to enumerate all my proofs. There is nothing in the human body that does not serve either for use or for ornament, and, what is most remarkable, we are all alike, and yet unlike; the generic resemblance does not preclude individual peculiarities. What of the mystery of birth, and the instinct by which the race is continued, and the process of lactation; are they not all from God? And God thought not only of the universal whole, but of each part also. Britain, for example, lacks sunshine, but is cheered by the warmth of the surrounding sea; the river Nile tempers the drought of Egypt; the Euphrates compensates Mesopotamia for the want of rain; the Indus is said to plant the Orient as well as to water it. Now, surely, if you go into a house and find everything neat and orderly and well-kept, you assume that it has a master, and that he himself is of more consequence than his property? So, in this house of the universe, when you consider the heavens and the earth, with every indication of forethought, order, and law, you may safely conclude that the lord and father of the universe is grander than the stars themselves or any part of the whole world. But perhaps, while there can be no doubt as to providence, you may not feel sure whether the heavenly domain is governed by the power of one king, or by the votes of several. This question may be elucidated by a reference to mundane kingdoms, which I suppose must be analogous. Now, has any partnership of a throne ever begun in good faith or ended without bloodshed? I say nothing of the Persian method of determining the succession by the augury of the neighing of horses, and I ignore the story of the Theban brothers as an obsolete fable. But the slaying of Remus in order that his twin brother might rule over a hut and a few shepherds is a well-known historical fact. Again, the wars between Pompey and his father-in-law, Caesar, went on over the whole world, and even a vast empire could not find room for them both. Notice also the parallel of bees, who have one leader, as has also every flock of sheep, and every herd of cattle. Can you conceive that in heaven the majesty and supremacy of true and divine empire are divided and shared, when it is evident that God, the father of all things, has neither beginning nor end; he who gives its origin to everything, but is himself eternal; who before the world was to himself in place of the world; who commands all things whatsoever by his word, regulates them by his wisdom, and perfects them by his goodness? He cannot be seen, for he is too bright for our eyes; neither can he be handled; nor appraised, for he is greater than our senses. He is infinite and immeasurable, and is known only to himself in all his greatness. Our own narrow intellects can only estimate him worthily when we say that he cannot be estimated. I hold, indeed, that he who thinks that he knows the greatness of God thereby lessens it, while he who refuses to lessen it does not know it. And seek no name for God. God is his name. Names are needed when individuals have to be distinguished from a multitude; but for God, who is alone, God is the one and only name. If I called him 'father,' you would think of him as of a natural father; if 'king,' you would connect him with an earthly kingdom; if 'lord,' you would surely deem him a mortal. But take away all that names connote, and you will realize his clear essence. As to that, I think everyone agrees with me. I listen to the common people; when they lift up their hands in prayer, 'God' is the only expression they use; 'God is great'; 'God is true'; and 'if God will give.' Is that the distinctive formula of the professing Christian, or the instinctive word of the people? I might add that those who regard Jupiter as supreme admit the unity of divine power, though they make a mistake in using that particular name.

"I find also that the poets speak of one father of gods and men, and say that 'the minds of mortals correspond to the fortune assigned to them by the parent of all.' What says Virgil, the Mantuan? Are not his words very clear, very near the mark, and very true? 'In the beginning,' says he, 'a spirit maintains the heaven and the land,' and the other parts of the universe, 'and a pervading mind actuates them. From it come men and cattle,' and all other living things. And in another passage he calls this mind and spirit 'God.' These are his words: 'For God goes through all the lands, and the tracts of the sea, and the profundity of heaven.' And how else do we describe God but as mind, and reason, and spirit? Let us examine, if you please, the teaching of philosophers, and you will find that, with formal differences, they are substantially united and agreed on this particular doctrine. I will not lay stress on those primitive thinkers whose fragmentary sayings led to their being called the Wise Men; but I must begin with Thales of Miletus as the first of all, and the first to discuss divine things. Thales said that water was the primal element, and that God was the intelligence that had made everything from it. Thus the theory of the earliest philosopher has at the root of it something in common with our own view. Anaximenes, and after him Diogenes of Apollonia, regard God as air, infinite and immeasurable. Here, again, is a similar agreement as to the divine nature. The God of Anaxagoras is said to be the manifestation and energy of an infinite intelligence; and the God of Pythagoras is a spirit moving in, and occupied with, all nature, from whom also the life of every living thing is derived. Xenophanes, as we know, taught that God is the infinite intelligent All; Antisthenes, that there were many popular gods, but one natural chief. Speusippus viewed God as the animate energy by which all things are directed. And Democritus, though he was the first discoverer of atoms, does he not generally speak of God as nature, which throws off images, and as intelligence? Straton says that he is nature, and the great Epicurus, who thought that the gods were either inactive or non-existent, makes nature supreme. Aristotle recognizes one power, but wavers, for sometimes he calls God intelligence, and sometimes the world, and sometimes he sets God over the world. Heraclides of Pontus in one way and another implies that there is divine intelligence in the world. Theophrastus also wavers; in one place he attributes superiority to the world, and in another to the divine mind. Zeno, Chrysippus, and Cleanthes, differing as they do, all ultimately return to the unity of providence. Cleanthes sometimes speaks of God as mind, soul, or ether, but generally as reason. Zeno, his master, holds that the law of nature is divine, and sometimes regards the ether, and sometimes reason, as the first cause of all things. When he explains Juno as the air, Jupiter as the heaven, Neptune as the sea, and Vulcan as fire, and shows that the other popular deities are only elements personified, he strikes a convincing blow at a vulgar error. In much the same way Chrysippus believes God to be divine power, reasoned nature, the order of the world, and necessity and destiny; and he follows Zeno in his interpretation of the cosmogony of Hesiod, Homer, and the Orphic songs. Diogenes of Babylon adopts the same principle of interpretation, and teaches that the delivery of Jupiter and the birth of Minerva, and the other myths, relate to natural, and not to supernatural, things. Xenophon, the pupil of Socrates, says that the form of the true God cannot be seen, and so ought not to be inquired into. Ariston the Stoic declares that God can by no means be comprehended. Both of them are rendered conscious of the majesty of God by the hopelessness of all attempts to understand him. Plato speaks still more clearly of God, and of the realities and names of things; his discourses would be altogether divine, but for an occasional base alloy of political prejudice. To Plato, in the 'Timaeus,' God, specifically called 'God,' is the parent of the world, the creator of the soul, the maker of things in the heavens and on the earth. It is difficult to find him because of his enormous and incredible might; 'and even if we found him, to tell of him to all men would be impossible.' These are virtually our own doctrines, for we know God and speak of him as the parent of all, and never publicly tell of him unless we are questioned.

"I have now enumerated the opinions of almost all the best-known philosophers. They all speak of one God, though under many different names, so that one might imagine either that the Christians of to-day are philosophers, or that the philosophers of old were Christians. Now, seeing that the world is ruled by providence, and governed by the will of one God, we must not assent to the polytheistic fables of the poets who pleased and ensnared the ancients. These are refuted by the opinions of their own philosophers, who have on their side the authority both of reason and of antiquity. Our ancestors had such a very easy faith in fiction that they illogically believed in all sorts of queer monsters and marvels, such as the composite Scylla, the multiform Chimaera, the Hydra whose wounds invigorated it and renewed its life, and the Centaurs, that were an amalgamation of horses and riders. In short, they were ready to swallow whatever popular fancy chose to invent. Why, they believed those preposterous fables of men being turned into birds and beasts, and trees and flowers; which miracles, if they ever did happen, might happen now; only they do not happen now, for the good reason that they cannot. In the same way as regards the gods, our simple ancestors were to the last degree ignorant and credulous. They paid religious honours to their kings, liked to see them again in their images when they were dead, tried to perpetuate their memory by statues, and made things which could only be comforting memorials into objects of worship. Also, before the world was opened up by commerce, and before the nations had adopted each other's rites and customs, each separate people worshipped its founder, or some famous general, or some chaste queen stronger than her sex, or the discoverer of some useful thing or art, or some citizen of happy memory. Thus the dead were honoured, and an example was given to posterity.

"Read what historians and wise men have written, and you will derive the same impression as myself. Euhemerus[12] proves that merit and benefactions went to the making of gods, and he enumerates their lineage, their countries, and their burial-places. He localizes them, as the Dictaean Jupiter, the Delphic Apollo, the Pharian Isis, and the Eleusinian Ceres. Prodicus says that those who benefited mankind by their discoveries were promoted to be gods. The philosopher Persaeus makes the same remark, and applies the same name to the discovery and to the discoverer, as in the comic proverb that 'Venus freezes without Bacchus and Ceres.' Alexander the

Great, of Macedon, told his mother in a famous letter that the priest had been intimidated into revealing to him the secret of these deified men. He puts Vulcan first of all the gods, and then the race of Jupiter. But Saturn was the first of all this tribe of gods, and all the writers of antiquity, both Greek and Roman, represent him as a man. The historians Nepos and Cassius admit this fact, and Thallus and Diodorus say the same. This Saturn was a refugee from Crete, and came to Italy to escape the wrath of his son. King Janus received him kindly, and, in return, like a polite Greek, he taught the rustic Italians a number of things, such as writing, the minting of money, and the making of implements. He named the country in which he lay hid Latium, and a city, Saturnia, was named after him, and the Janiculum from Janus, so both he and Janus immortalized themselves. Undoubtedly, this refugee, Saturn, was a man, the father of a man, and the son of a man. He was called the son of Earth or Heaven because the Italians did not know his parentage, just as in the present day we say that people whom we see unexpectedly are sent from heaven, while those whose origin is obscure or unknown are called sons of the earth. His son Jupiter, after he had turned out his father, reigned over Crete, died there, and had sons there. The cave of Jupiter is still visited, and his sepulchre is shown, and his human origin is implied in the rites with which he is worshipped. But I need not explain all these divinities individually, one after another. The human character of the first generation has been proved, and must have been transmitted to the descendants. Perhaps, however, you may suggest that they became gods after death, as Romulus was a god, because Proculus falsely swore to it, and Juba, because the Moors made him one, and the other kings who have been deified, not so much to create a belief in their divinity as to do honour to well-used power. I may remark, by the way, that these personages have no wish to be deified. They would rather remain as men, and are afraid of deification, even when they are old. But you cannot in reality make gods out of dead men, for God cannot die, nor from anyone who is born, for all who are born die. That only is divine which has neither beginning nor end. And if the gods were born, why are no gods born now? Perhaps Jupiter is too old; perhaps Juno has ceased to bear children; perhaps Minerva has grown gray before becoming a mother? Or has the family come to an end because people do not believe in these fables? Why, if the gods could multiply, but could not die, we should have more gods than men, and heaven and air and earth could not contain them. Clearly, they were not gods, but men, whose birth we read of, and whom we know to be dead.

"Consider also the sacred rites and the mysteries themselves. They are full of tragedy, and fate, and death, and woe, and lamentations of unhappy deities. Isis, with Cynocephalus and the shaven priests, laments for her son, who is lost and cannot be found. Her priests beat their breasts, and mimic the sorrow of the wretched mother; and then, when the boy is found, Isis rejoices, the priests jump for joy, and Cynocephalus is very proud of having found him. Regularly every year they repeat this hide and seek, this ridiculous weeping worship. And these rites, which were originally Egyptian, have now become Roman also. Ceres, with burning torches, and girt with a serpent, anxiously follows up the footprints of the ravished Proserpine. These are the Eleusinian rites. And what are the rites of Jupiter? A she-goat is his nurse, and he is taken away from his voracious father lest he should be eaten, and the cymbals of the Corybantes keep up a jingling noise, so that his father may not hear the child's crying. As for the rites of Cybele, I should be ashamed to describe them.[13] They are not in reality sacred rites, but tortures. And what of the physical appearance and dress of your gods; are they not absurd and degrading? Vulcan is a lame and weak god; Apollo, even as a grown man, has not a hair on his face, while Aesculapius, though he is the son of the young Apollo, has a full beard. Neptune has blue eyes, Minerva gray; Juno is ox-eyed. Mercury has wings on his feet; Pan hoofs; Saturn fetters. Janus has two faces, as if he now and then walked backwards. Diana the huntress is short-kilted, but Diana of the Ephesians is provided with breasts many and fruitful; and Diana of the Cross-ways inspires awe with three heads and many hands. And your great Jupiter himself is represented sometimes with a beard and sometimes without; surname him Ammon, and he has horns; Capitolinus, and he wields thunderbolts; Latiaris, and he is smeared with blood; Feretrius, and he wears a crown.[14] In short, there are as many grotesque Jupiters as there are names for him. Erigone hanged herself in order to appear as the constellation Virgo; the twins, Castor and Pollux, live by dying alternately; Aesculapius is struck by lightning in order that he may become a god; and Hercules rids himself of mortality in the flames of Oeta.

"These blundering fables we learn from our ignorant parents, and, what is more serious, we inculcate them in our literature. In particular, our poets have used all their authority to injure the cause of truth. For that reason, Plato excluded Homer from his ideal republic, in spite of his distinction and his laurels. Homer especially introduces your gods, playfully, it may be, among the human combatants and the human interests in the Trojan war. He arrays one against the other, wounds Venus; binds, wounds, and puts to flight Mars; and he relates that Jupiter was released by Briareus to prevent him from being bound by the other deities, and that he shed tears of blood for his son Sarpedon, whom he could not save from death. Elsewhere, we have Hercules cleaning out a stable, and Apollo tending sheep for Admetus. Neptune built walls for Laomedon, and the unlucky workman was never paid for his work. In Homer, Jupiter's thunderbolt is forged on the anvil, together with the arms of Aeneas, though the heaven and the thunder and lightning existed long before Jupiter's birth in Crete, and the Cyclops could not imitate, and Jupiter could not but dread, the true fire of lightning. What need I say of the stories of Mars and Venus, and of Ganymede? All these fables are related in order that precedents may be found for the vices of mankind. Young people are corrupted by these artistic fictions and lies; they grow up with a firm belief in them, and unhappily become old men with these same notions still in their heads, though the truth is clear enough, if only one looks for it. Who can doubt, then, that, if the common people pray to the consecrated images of these gods, and publicly worship them, it is because their ignorance is deluded by the glamour of art, the glitter of gold, the sheen of silver, and the radiance of ivory? But if a man only considered the processes and contrivances by which every image is manufactured, he would blush at the thought of fearing the raw material which the workman has bullied into the shape of a god.[15] Your wooden god, taken perhaps from the remains of a funeral pile, or a gibbet, is fixed up, and cut, and chipped, and planed. Your brazen or silver god, often made out of some unclean vessel, as was done by the Egyptian king, is melted down, and hammered and fashioned on an anvil. Your stone god is carved and scraped and polished by some low fellow, and is equally unconscious of these early insults and of the honours afterwards paid to him. But perhaps the stone, or wood, or silver is not as yet a god? Well, but when does it become a god? It is cast, or carved, or chiselled; and still it is not a god. It is soldered, and put together, and set up on a pedestal, and it is not a god even then. But when it is decorated, and consecrated, and prayed to, then at last it really is a god; that is, when some man calls it a god, and dedicates it.

"How much more accurately the instinct of dumb animals takes your gods for what they are worth! The mice and the swallows and the kites know that they cannot feel, and nibble at them, and attack them, and light on them, and nest in their very mouths if you do not drive them away. Spiders come and spin their webs over your gods' faces, and hang their threads from their noses, so that you have continually to clean and dust and rub up your helpless but revered handiwork. Meanwhile, it does not occur to any of you that you ought to know what the god is before you worship him; you all blindly follow your fathers, and would rather err with them than think for yourselves; you know nothing, none of you, of the gods whom you fear. Hence your gold and silver images are nothing but holy bullion, and the shapes of your foolish statues are only conventional;—and hence comes your Roman superstition. If you examine its forms and ceremonies, how many of them are ridiculous and even distressing! Some of the worshippers go half naked in midwinter, others go about in hats, carrying round old shields, beating drums, and parading the images of the gods as they beg from street to street. Some of the shrines you may enter once a year, others you may not enter at all. Some ceremonies are for women only, others only for men; and there are others again where the presence of a slave renders an expiation necessary. Then there are rites for which unchastity is a qualification, or which involve ceremonial self-mutilation.[16] Anyone can see that these are the follies of diseased and depraved minds, in which a multitude of insane people aid and abet one another. In this case, the numbers of the madmen is the excuse for the general madness.

"But you urge that this same superstition gave the Romans their power, and increased it and strengthened it, and that they became mighty not so much by their valour as by their religion and their devotion. Truly, our wonderful and noble Roman justice was forecast in the very cradle of the infant empire! As a matter of fact, our infant empire was begotten in crime and maintained by terrorism. Our first commons—ruffians, criminals, profligates, assassins and traitors—congregated together in what was a city of refuge; and their leader and ruler, Romulus, by way of acquiring an infamous pre-eminence, murdered his own brother. In this manner our most religious state was inaugurated. Then a number of young women, some of them promised and betrothed, and some married, were lawlessly carried off and appropriated, and in the war that ensued with their fathers, kindred blood, that is, of fathers-in-law, was poured out. Where can you find a more impious, a more audacious, a more cynical piece of wickedness? To drive their neighbours from their land, to destroy the nearest cities, with their temples and altars, to lead their enemies captive, to wax strong by the ruin of others and their own villainy, was the common policy of Romulus and the other kings, and of your later generals. All that the Romans hold and worship and possess is the result of bare-faced robbery. All your temples have been built out of the sack and ruin of cities, after despoiling their gods and slaughtering their priests. It is adding insult to injury to serve a beaten religion, and to pray to your captives after a victory over them. To adore the gods whom you have taken by force does them no honour, but only sanctifies sacrilege. But every Roman triumph has involved an act of impiety, every trophy has been stolen from your enemies' gods. I should say that the Romans became great, not through religion, but because their sacrilege went unpunished. Besides, how could these gods, whom they had conquered and begun to worship, help the

Romans, when they had not been able to do anything for their own people? We know who the native Roman deities were. The gods of Romulus were Picus, Tiberinus, Consus, Pilumnus, and Volumnus. Tatius invented and worshipped Cloacina; Hostilius added Pavor and Pallor. Soon afterwards, Febris was made a goddess by somebody or other; such was the superstition fostered in that city of fever and illness. And I suppose that Acca Laurentia and Flora, most disreputable persons, both of them, may be reckoned among the deities, and the diseases, of the Romans. So these were the personages who advanced the Roman power in the teeth of the gods of the other nations! Mars of Thrace, Jupiter of Crete, Juno of Argos, of Samos, of Carthage, Diana of Tauris, the Idaean Mother, and the monsters—I cannot call them the gods—of Egypt could do nothing against them! But possibly the Roman priests were more holy, and the priestesses more pure? Far from it. That at any rate cannot be maintained.[17] After all, before your native gods were heard of, there were for a long time under God's dispensation the empires of the Assyrians, the Medes, the Persians, the Greeks, and the

Egyptians, though they had no Pontifices and Arvales and Salii and Vestals and Augurs, and did not decide affairs of state according to the appetite of a coop of poultry.

"This brings me to the subject of Roman auspices and auguries. You have given carefully chosen instances of disaster following the neglect of them and of good fortune attending their observance. According to you, Claudius and Flaminius and Junius lost armies because they did not think fit to wait until the fowls showed by their feeding that the moment was favourable. But what of Regulus? Did not he regard the auguries, and was not he captured? Mancinus did nothing irreligious, but he had to pass under the yoke and surrender. Paulus, again, had the good augury of hungry birds, yet he was overthrown, and with him the greater part of our manhood, at Cannae. When the auguries and auspices indicated that Caius Caesar should not send his fleet over to Africa before the winter, he ignored them, and crossed over and conquered all the more easily. And what shall I say, or rather, what might I not say, in speaking of oracles? After his death, there was an oracle of Amphiaraus which foretold the future, though while he was living he had not foreseen that his wife would betray him for the sake of a necklace. Tiresias had visions; a blind man who could not see his everyday surroundings. Ennius invented the reply of the Pythian Apollo about Pyrrhus, because at that time Apollo had ceased from his mystic utterances; the cautious and ambiguous oracle failed as soon as men became more civilized and less credulous. And Demosthenes, because he knew that a certain oracular response was manufactured, charged the oracle with being in the pay of his enemy. But now and then, no doubt, both auspices and oracles have happened to be true; they have told many lies, but sometimes the event has chanced to corroborate them. I will try to get to the bottom of this delusion, and to throw the clearest possible light upon this wicked darkness. There are false and vagrant spirits whose heavenly strength has perished under the weight of earthly sins and desires.[18] These spirits are immersed in wickedness, and ever seek to console themselves for their lost original purity by involving others in their ruin, their depravity, and their alienation from God. The poets recognize them as 'daemons;' philosophers discuss them, and

Socrates knew a familiar daemon at whose prompting he abstained from or undertook affairs. The Magi, too, not only know the daemons, but owe all their magical powers to them. They perform their tricks by their help and inspiration, when they make non-existent things visible, and existing things invisible. Of those Magi, the first in eloquence and activity is Hostanes. He pays due honour to the true God, and knows that the angels, his ministers and messengers, guard his habitation, and while they wait on him in worship tremble at his will and countenance. This Hostanes has attested the fact that the daemons are earthly, wandering beings, the enemies of mankind. And what says Plato, who thought it hard to discover God, but has no difficulty in speaking of angels and daemons? Does he not try in the 'Symposium' to explain the nature of daemons? He holds that there is a substance intermediate between the mortal and the immortal, a compound of earthly matter and heavenly imponderability; and from this, he says, comes Eros, who takes possession of men's minds and senses and produces in them their passions and affections and desires.

"Now, these unclean spirits, the daemons, as is shown by the Magi and the philosophers, shelter themselves in consecrated statues and images, and inspire them with the authority of a present deity. They prompt the soothsayers, haunt the shrines, generally manage the omens, direct the flight of the birds, rule the casting of lots, and invent oracles with an ounce of truth in a bushel of falsehood. They are at once deceivers and deceived, since they know not the pure truth, and such of it as they do know they will not confess to their own destruction. Thus they degrade men, and turn them away from heaven towards material things. They cross their lives, disquiet their sleep, and entering into them unawares, like impalpable spirits, produce diseases and mental torture and physical deformity in order to compel men to worship them. Finally, when they have battened on the steaming sacrifices of the altars, they leave off tormenting their victims in order that they may have the credit of the cure. Credit them also with the fanatical priests whom you see running about in the streets, raving and behaving like Bacchanals actually outside the temple. It is the same demoniac impulse, only with a different manifestation. To the daemons again are referable the legends you have mentioned of the renewal of the games in Jupiter's honour in consequence of a dream, of the apparition of the Twin Brethren on horseback, and of the vessel that was hauled by a matron's girdle. Most of your own people know that the daemons confess to all this whenever they are driven forth from men's bodies by the scourge and fire of our words. Saturn himself, and Serapis, and Jupiter, and all the daemons whom you worship, confess what they are when they are thus overcome, and surely the disgraceful truth, told in the presence of a number of your people, is no lie. You may believe their own testimony that they are daemons. For when they are adjured by the true and only God, the wretches involuntarily shudder within the bodies they occupy, and either come forth at once, or gradually vanish, according to the faith of the patient and the grace of the healer. Consequently, they shun the Christians at close quarters, though at a safe distance from our meetings they harass us through your agency. They possess the minds of the ignorant and secretly inspire them to hate us, and work upon their fears; for it is natural to hate, and, if you can, to injure those whom you fear. Therefore they harden men's minds, and prejudice them against us in order that people may hate us before they know us, and may neither follow us nor remain neutral.

"You must believe me when I say from my own sad experience how unjust it is to form an opinion, as you do, on things which you do not know and have not investigated. Formerly I did the same, and believed as blindly as yourself that the Christians worshipped monsters, ate children, and held licentious feasts. I did not realize that, thanks to the daemons, these fables were always in the air, but were never examined and inquired into, and that in all that length of time no one ever came forward to betray the Christians, though he would have been rewarded as well as pardoned; the fact being that a Christian had nothing to blush for or to fear, but regretted only that he had not been converted earlier. And so, while we defended and protected the profane, the vicious, and the violent, we gave the Christians no fair hearing; and sometimes, when they confessed their faith, out of sheer pity for them we used to torture them that they might save themselves by denying it. In this way our wrongheaded inquisition was intended not to elicit the truth, but to compel a lie. And if anyone, weaker than the rest, and broken down by torture, denied that he was a Christian, we used to favour him as having purged all his misdeeds by his recantation and denial. You see, our ideas and conduct in the matter were exactly like your own. But if commonsense had governed these proceedings, instead of the influence of daemons, the proper course would have been, not to urge these men to deny Christianity, but to induce them to confess to profligacy, profanity, and the murder of children; these being the false charges with which the daemons, in their endeavours to raise an outcry against us, had filled the ears of our ignorant enemies. But what we did was only natural, for the rumour that lives on lies, and perishes when the truth is known, is the work of the daemons, who, in fact, are always spreading and fostering falsehood. From them comes the report you mention, that we regard the head of an ass as a holy thing. But who would be so foolish as to do that, or so much more foolish as to believe such a story? You however do consecrate asses in their stables in connexion with Vesta or Epona, and you decorate asses in the religious rites of Isis; you sacrifice and worship the heads of oxen and sheep, you hallow gods that are half goats and half men, and gods with the faces of lions and dogs. You adore and feed the bull Apis, like the Egyptians. You tolerate the Egyptian worship of serpents, crocodiles, and wild beasts generally, the slaying of any one of which gods is punishable by death. The other foul charge against us originates in the fouler imaginations and fouler habits of those who make it.[19]

"These shocking allegations are such as we ought not to notice, and in most cases it would be to our discredit to defend ourselves. You charge virtuous and clean-living people with conduct that would have been inconceivable had not you yourselves proved the contrary. When you say that a criminal and his cross are objects of our worship, you wander very far from the truth. You fancy that a criminal might merit, and an earthly being might succeed in inducing, a belief in his divinity. If so, he is indeed to be pitied whose whole hope is fixed on a mortal man, for with the death of that man his only help has perished. But the Egyptians really do choose a man to worship. They propitiate him alone, consult him about everything, and sacrifice to him. He is supreme, a god to others, but human enough to himself, whether he likes it or not, for, though others may be deluded, he cannot impose upon himself. Princes and kings, again, are treated not as great and exceptional men, which would be proper enough, but are falsely and disgracefully flattered as though they were gods. To the great, honour is due; to the good, love is the more acceptable tribute. However, people address these royal deities, pray to their images, and invoke their spirits, that is, their daemons; and it is safer to swear falsely by Jupiter than by the king. Again, we do not worship crosses, and we do not wish them to be worshipped. But you worship wooden gods, and so perhaps adore wooden crosses when they form part of your gods. After all, your ensigns and military standards are practically crosses, gilt and ornamented, and your trophies of victory are not only in the shape of a simple cross, but have something of the semblance of a man fixed upon them.[20] And surely the cross occurs naturally in the case of a ship under full sail, or when it glides along with its oars outspread; and the sign of a cross is made whenever a crossbeam is set up, and whenever a man stretches out his hands in pure prayer. The sign of the cross, therefore, is a fact in nature, and an element of your own religion.

"I wish I had here the man who asserts or believes that our initiation is by the blood of slaughtered infants. Can you really think that the practice exists among us of murdering tender babes and drinking their young blood? No one can possibly credit it, unless he is himself equal to such wickedness. Your people, however, sometimes expose new-born children to beasts and birds of prey, and sometimes strangle them, and sometimes kill them before they are born. These customs only follow the precedents set by your own gods. Saturn did not expose his children, but he ate them, and in many parts of Africa children were appropriately sacrificed to him by their parents, who smothered their cries by endearments and kisses so as not to offer a weeping victim. With the people of the Taurian Chersonese, and with the Egyptian

Busiris, it was the custom to immolate strangers, and the Gauls offered human, or, rather, inhuman sacrifices to Mercury. The Romans themselves have been known sacrificially to bury alive a Greek man and a Greek woman, and a Gaul of either sex; and even in the present day Jupiter Latiaris is worshipped with manslaughter, and, as becomes a son of Saturn, is fed on the blood of some base criminal. I believe that this same Jupiter taught Catiline the covenant of blood, taught Bellona to stain her rites by draughts of human blood, and taught people to cure epilepsy by blood; a remedy worse than the disease. Very similar is the conduct of those who eat the bloodstained animals of the arena after their meal of human flesh. But as for us, we have no part in the slaughter of men either as spectators or auditors, and so scrupulous are we as regards blood that we do not consider the blood even of cattle to be fit for food.

"As for the allegation that our common feasts are scenes of debauchery, that is an enormous invention of the whole lying assemblage of daemons, who try to stain our credit for purity with an infamous aspersion in order that people may be disgusted with us before they find out the truth. What your friend Fronto said on that subject was not the testimony of a witness, but the professional slander of an orator. Such scandals occur rather among your own people. Are the marriage laws pure in Persia, Egypt, and Athens? Are your traditional histories pure, and the tragedies you admire, and your gods, and, for the matter of that, yourselves?[21] On the other hand, we show our modesty, if not in our faces, in our souls. A Christian has either one duly married wife, or none. Our feasts are not only pure, but moderate. We have no great delicacies, and do not linger over our wine, but temper our mirth with sobriety. Pure in speech, and even more so in person, many of us willingly remain in single life without boasting of it. So far, indeed, are we from unchastity, that some of us shrink conscientiously even from lawful marriage. Nor do we consist entirely of the lowest classes, though we do refuse your official honours and decorations. Neither are we disloyal if both in our peaceful meetings and separately we pursue the same good object. Neither are we 'talkative in secret corners' if you are ashamed or afraid to hear us in public. As for the daily increase of our numbers, that does not suggest that we are in error, but is evidence in our favour, for it shows that the good life retains its hold on its own people and attracts others."[22] Again, we recognize each other, not, as you say, by some outward sign, but only by the mark of innocence and modesty. We love one another, apparently to your regret, because we have not learned to hate; and we call each other 'brother,' which you seem to object to, because all of us are the children of one God and father, comrades in faith, and coheirs in hope. But your people have mutual hatred instead of mutual recognition, and fratricide is your only acknowledgement of brotherhood.

"Do you really imagine that we conceal the object of our worship because we have no shrines and altars? What image can I possibly make of God when man himself, rightly regarded, is God's image? And what temple shall I build for him when the whole world, his handiwork, cannot contain him? Shall I, who have a more spacious dwelling myself, though I am only a man, try to inclose him within the four walls of one small building? Is he not better hallowed in the soul, and consecrated in the inmost heart? Shall I offer as victims and sacrifices to God the things which he has given me for my use, and so fling back his gift? That would be ungrateful. The fit sacrifice is a good spirit, a pure mind, and a clear conscience. He, then, who follows after innocence prays to God; he who pursues righteousness sacrifices to God; he who abstains from deceit propitiates God; he who saves a fellow-man from peril offers the chiefest victim. These are our sacrifices, these are the sacred rites of our God. With us, the most upright man is the most religious. But, as you say, we neither show to others, nor ourselves see, the God whom we worship. In truth, it is a reason for believing him to be God, that we can perceive, but cannot see him. In his works, and in all the forces of nature, in thunder, in lightning, and in the unclouded blue, we see his ever-present power. You need not wonder that you cannot see God himself. Winds and storms blow and shake everything, but the winds are not actually visible to the eyes. It is the sun that enables us to see everything;

but you cannot look into the sun, for his rays dull your sight, and, if you persevere in the attempt, you see nothing at all. Do you think that you could bear to gaze at the maker of the sun, the very source of light, when you have to turn away from the lightning and hide from the thunderbolts? Do you expect to see God with your physical eyes, while your soul, which gives you life and speech, is invisible and intangible? You have urged that God does not heed the actions of men, and that from his place in heaven he cannot at once pervade the whole and regard individuals. Man, you are mistaken and deceived. From what place can God be far distant when all the regions of heaven and earth, and all beyond our earthly sphere, are filled with him who made them? In every place he is not only very near to us, but is mingled with us. To take another illustration from the sun, it is set high in the heavens, but it throws its light over all lands, and diffuses its beams everywhere with unfailing glory. Much more is God, the author of all things, the observer of all men, and from whom no secrets are hid, present in darkness, and in that other darkness of our thoughts. Not only do we live under his eye, but I may almost say we live with him.

"We do not take credit to ourselves for our numbers. Many as we may seem to be to ourselves, we are very few in the sight of God. Men make their human distinctions of race and nation, but to God the whole world is one household. Kings know the affairs of their kingdoms only through their ministers: God has no need to be so informed, seeing that we live not only in his sight, but, so to speak, in his bosom. You say that it has not helped the Jews to worship one God with altars, and temples, and the utmost veneration. You are making a mistake if you forget or do not know their early history and recall only their later misfortunes. They had reason to know the strength and power of our God—for he is the same God of all—and as long as they worshipped him in purity, innocence, and holiness, as long as they kept his wholesome laws, they became a multitude instead of a handful, rich instead of poor, rulers instead of slaves; and at the bidding of God, the elements fighting for them, a few unarmed men overthrew and pursued great armies. Read their books, or, if you prefer Roman writers, pass from more ancient records and see what Flavius Josephus and Antonius Julianus say of the Jews; then you will find that they brought their misfortunes upon themselves by their wickedness, and that nothing happened to them which was not predicted in the event of persistent disobedience. They deserted God before he deserted them, and they were not, in your profane phrase, 'captured with their God,' but were surrendered by him as renegades from his teaching.

"Now, with regard to the burning of the world, it is a vulgar error to hold that there cannot be an unexpected conflagration or a failure of moisture. No philosopher doubts that everything that has a beginning has also an end, and that all created things perish. The Stoics uniformly think that the heavens with all that they contain will be overcome by fire whenever the springs of water fail them, and that the world itself will take fire when all the moisture has been used up.[23] The Epicureans agree with them as to the conflagration of the elements and the wreck of the universe. Plato speaks to a like effect; he says that parts of the world are alternately flooded and alternately overheated, and, though he describes the world as having been made eternal and imperishable, he adds that God alone, its maker, can unmake it. What wonder, then, if this massive structure of ours should be destroyed by its builder? And so with the renewal of life, the best philosophers, from Pythagoras downwards, and especially Plato, have held it with a sort of imperfect and partial belief. They say that after the dissolution of the body the soul alone remains eternally, and finds new habitations; and they so far pervert the truth as to suggest that the souls of men migrate into birds and beasts. That idea is more suitable for pantomime than for philosophy. However, it is enough for my purpose that on the general question your philosophers do to some extent agree with us. And surely, no one would be so dull or so stupid as to deny that God, who made man originally, can make him again and afresh? If he was born from nothing, so he can be renewed from nothing, for renewal must needs be less difficult than creation. Do you believe that that which is withdrawn from our dull eyes is necessarily dead in God's sight also? Every human body, whether it becomes dry dust, or moisture, or a handful of ashes, or thin vapour, is removed from us, but is reserved for the purposes of God, who guards the elements. Nor, as you suppose, do we fear that our dead will be prejudiced if they are not buried; it is only that we prefer burial to cremation as being the older and better custom. But see how all nature offers us consolatory suggestions of a future resurrection. The sun sets and rises again, the stars sink and return, flowers wither and grow again, shrubs grow green after their old age, seeds cannot spring up except they perish. So the body in its sepulchre is like trees in winter, which show no sign of sap and seem quite dry. You are not so impatient as to expect a tree to grow green in midwinter; and we in like manner wait for the spring-time of the body. I am aware that many men, conscious of their misdeeds, rather wish than believe that death may prove annihilation. They would rather be snuffed out altogether than survive and be punished. They are in error, and the more so because of their long impunity and the extreme patience of God, whose judgement is equally just and tardy. And yet men are warned by philosophers and poets alike of the infernal river of fire, with its encompassing flames; and so terrible is it that even their king Jupiter swears solemn oaths by its scorching banks and its dreadful depths, foreseeing and fearing the punishment of himself and his worshippers. Of those torments there is no limit nor end. There the cunning fire roasts and restores the limbs, wastes and refreshes them. And just as lightning may strike the body without consuming it, and the flames of Aetna and Vesuvius and other volcanoes burn and are never spent, so that penal fire does not make an end of those on whom it feeds, but is maintained by their continuing torture. That the punishment is deserved by those who know not God, such as the impious and the wicked, no one can doubt without profanity. It must be as wrong not to recognize the father and lord of all as to oppose him. And although ignorance of God is punishable, even as the knowledge of him helps to procure pardon, yet[24] ... our Christian morality, lax as our system is in some respects, will be found on comparison much better than your own. For instance, your people forbid adultery, but practise it, while we are true husbands all our lives; you punish crimes when they have been committed, with us the mere contemplation of them is sinful; you fear your accomplices, we fear conscience alone, of which we cannot divest ourselves. Besides, the gaols are full of your people, but no Christian who is not an apostate is to be found there, except on account of his religion.

"Let no one attempt to comfort himself, or excuse the results of his life, by the doctrine of fate. For, granting an element of luck in our circumstances, still the mind is free, and consequently a man is judged by his acts and not by his position. And what is fate but the determination of God with regard to each one of us? God, who has a foreknowledge of human nature, determines the destinies of individuals according to their deserts. It is not our birth, then, that is visited upon us, but the evil character of our nature that is punished. On this subject let this slight remark serve for the present; we may discuss it more fully at some other time. I turn to another matter. It is not to our discredit, but just the reverse, if most of us are reputed to be poor. Luxury relaxes the mind, poverty braces it. Besides, who can be poor if he wants nothing, if he does not envy his neighbour, if he is rich towards God? You should rather call a man poor if he has a great deal and wants more. After all, nobody can possibly be as poor as when he is born. The birds and the cattle have no incomes, but

ERRATUM.

P. 73, line 23, for *disease* read *disuse*.

spires fortitude, adversity often teaches courage, and both mental and bodily powers grow rusty with disease and idleness. Your own famous men, by the way, whom you have had occasion to mention, all came to greatness through suffering. It is not that God cannot help us or despises us, for he rules all and crimes when they have been committed, with us the mere contemplation of them is sinful; you fear your accomplices, we fear conscience alone, of which we cannot divest ourselves. Besides, the gaols are full of your people, but no Christian who is not an apostate is to be found there, except on account of his

punished. On this subject let this slight remark serve for the present; we may discuss it more fully at some other time. I turn to another matter. It is not to our discredit, but just the reverse, if most of us are reputed to be poor. Luxury relaxes the mind, poverty braces it. Besides, who can be poor if he wants nothing, if he does not envy his neighbour, if he is rich towards God? You should rather call a man poor if he has a great deal and wants more. After all, nobody can possibly be as poor as when he is born. The birds and the cattle have no incomes, but they find their daily food; and all these are ours, to possess and to use in moderation. Just as the man with the lightest burden goes easiest on the road, so the happiest man in the journey through life is he who is cheerful with a light purse and does not groan under the weight of riches. We would ask God for comforts, if we thought them desirable, and he who owns all would, no doubt, give us a part; but our ideals of innocency, patience, and virtue lead us to despise, and not to acquire, wealth. As for our experience of human infirmity, it is no punishment to us, but a species of training. Infirmity inspires fortitude, adversity often teaches courage, and both mental and bodily powers grow rusty with disease and idleness. Your own famous men, by the way, whom you have had occasion to mention, all came to greatness through suffering. It is not that God cannot help us or despises us, for he rules all and loves his own; but he tests every man by adversity, tries every man's character by dangers, and examines it down to the very day of death, knowing that in his sight nothing can perish. As gold is assayed by fire, so are we proved by perils.

"How noble a spectacle it must be in God's sight when a Christian does battle with pain, and is matched like a gladiator against threats and torments and tortures; when he laughs at the terrors and din of the fatal theatre and offers himself to the executioner; when he asserts his liberty against kings and princes, and yields only to God, whose he is; and when, with the triumphant air of a conqueror, he beards the very man who pronounced sentence upon him! He is indeed a conqueror, for he has won that for which he fought. What soldier does not adventure himself the more bravely under the eye of his general? But the reward comes only after the deed of valour, and if the soldier is killed, the earthly general cannot give what he has not got;—he cannot prolong the man's life, but can only honour his good service. But the soldier of God is not deserted in trouble, nor put an end to by death. The Christian may seem unhappy, but cannot be so in reality. You yourselves laud to the skies the behaviour of unfortunate people like Mucius Scaevola, who, when he made a mistake and failed to kill the king, would have lost his life if he had not voluntarily sacrificed his right hand. But how many of our folk have borne in silence the burning, not of the right hand, but of the whole body, and that, too, when it was in their power to procure their release? Need I compare our grown men to Mucins and Aquilius and Regulus? Why, our boys and girls are so inspired to bear pain that they make light of crucifixion, wild beasts, and all the tortures and penalties of the law. You wretched people, you do not understand that no one submits to pain voluntarily without good reason, or can endure torture without God's help. What misleads you, perhaps, is the fact that the godless are rich and honoured and powerful. So much the worse for them. They are raised the higher that they may have the greater fall. They are as victims fattened for slaughter and garlanded for sacrifice, and some of them are raised to high places in order that the natural madness of an abandoned soul may have full play.[25] But where is true happiness without God? When death come, it eludes us like a dream, before it is grasped. Are you a king? Your fears will be in proportion to the fear that you inspire, and, for all your guards, you will be alone in the hour of danger. Are you rich? It is not well to trust to fortune, and life's short road is made none the easier, but is only burdened, by your money-bags. Are you proud of your official dignities? It is a poor and mistaken ambition to swagger in purple while your soul wants a wash. Are you noble by birth and ancestry? We are all equal at birth, and virtue is the only true distinction. We, then, who value virtue and modesty necessarily have no part or lot in your evil pleasures and pomps and shows. We know how they originated from your ritual, and we condemn their dangerous attractions. And who can help condemning the disreputable excitements of the circus, and the organized teaching of murder in your gladiatorial shows? In your stage-plays also there is just as much wild passion, but more long-drawn-out infamy. The obscenities of the actor dishonour your own gods,[26] and his sham tears evoke your sympathy, so that, while you insist on real murder in the arena, you deplore the imitation of it on the stage.

"Once more, our refusal of meat and drink that has been offered on your altars is not a confession of weakness, but an assertion of true liberty. For though everything that is produced is the pure gift of God, still we reject these things in order that no one may suppose that we are making any concession to the daemons to whom they are offered, or that we are ashamed of our religion. As to flowers, it is well known that we use and enjoy them; spring roses and lilies and all that have fine colours and sweet scents. We use them both scattered about and as ornaments for the neck. You must excuse us for not crowning our heads with them; we prefer to enjoy their scent in the usual way, and not to waste their sweetness on our heads and our hair. It is true also that we do not place wreaths on our dead. In truth, I am rather surprised at your own custom; you burn a corpse on the hypothesis that it cannot feel, and you crown it on the contrary supposition, although the dead man does not want flowers if he is happy, and cannot enjoy them if he is not. However, our funeral rites are adorned by the same tranquillity as our lives. We weave no perishable crowns, but obtain from God a living crown of eternal flowers. Quietly and humbly, and with confidence in God's goodness, we cherish our hope of future happiness by our faith in his ever-present majesty. So do we rise again in bliss, and live already in the contemplation of the future. Socrates must look out for himself;—the Athenian buffoon who admitted that he knew nothing, though he was proud of the prompting of his most untrustworthy daemon. Arcesilaus and Carneades and Pyrrho, and all the multitude of Academics, may deliberate as long as they like, and Simonides may postpone his decision indefinitely, for all I care. We despise the pride of the philosophers, whom we know to be misleaders and flatterers [27] of the great, notwithstanding their eloquent censure of their own faults. For ourselves, we wear our wisdom not in our dress, but in our minds; we do not say great things, but do them; and we glory in having attained that which the philosophers, with all their diligent search, could not find. How can we be thankless and discontented if the truth of God has borne fruit in our own time? Let us enjoy our good fortune, and direct our minds aright so that superstition may be restrained, impiety banished, and the true faith upheld."

When Octavius had done speaking, we sat still for a minute or two, too much surprised to say anything. For myself, I was reduced to silence by my extreme admiration for the arguments, the instances, and the wide reading with which he had illustrated what it is much easier to feel than to express. I admired also the way in which he had turned against his opponents their own philosophical weapons, and had shown that truth was such as it was easy to understand and to welcome.

Caecilius was the first to speak, and interrupted my reflections by saying: " I congratulate my friend Octavius most heartily, and myself too, and I need not wait for the verdict. We have won, as things are, and I say 'we' because I am unprincipled enough to claim a share in the victory; for if Octavius has overcome me, I have got the better of my errors. As for the main question, I admit what he has said of providence and the unity of God, and I agree with him as to the merits of what is now the sect of both of us. But as it is past midday, let us reserve for to-morrow certain matters, not serious objections, on which I should like fuller information. The inquiry will be all the easier for our being agreed in principle."

"For the sake of all three of us," said I, "I am delighted with the happy result; with my friend Octavius's victory, and with my own escape from the invidious duty of delivering judgement. I will not attempt to reward him with mere words of praise; and, besides, the testimony of man—especially of one man—would be inconclusive. But he has a noble reward from God, to whose inspiration and help he owes his eloquence and his success."

After this we parted in good spirits and good humour; Caecilius rejoicing that he had become a believer, and Octavius because he had made him one; and I for both reasons.

NOTES

NOTE I, page 3, line 4.

SERAPIS, or Osiris, was one of the Egyptian deities which, as Minucius says in another passage, had become Roman also. In his second chapter, Gibbon writes: "Rome, the capital of a great monarchy, was incessantly filled with subjects and strangers from every part of the world, who all introduced and enjoyed the favourite superstitions of their native country. Every city in the empire was justified in maintaining the purity of its ancient ceremonies; and the Roman senate, using the common privilege, sometimes interposed to check this inundation of foreign rites. The Egyptian superstition, of all the most contemptible and abject, was frequently prohibited; the temples of Serapis and Isis demolished, and their worshippers banished from Rome and Italy. But the zeal of fanaticism prevailed over the cold and feeble efforts of policy. The exiles returned, the proselytes multiplied, the temples were restored with increasing splendour, and Isis and Serapis at length assumed their place among the Roman deities. Nor was this indulgence a departure from the old maxims of government. In the purest ages of the commonwealth, Cybele and Aesculapius had been invited by solemn embassies; and it was customary to tempt the protectors of besieged cities by the promise of more distinguished honours than they possessed in their native country. Rome gradually became the common temple of her subjects; and the freedom of the city was bestowed on all the gods of mankind."

NOTE 2, page 12, line 11.

This reference to the Parthians is part of the internal evidence as to the date of the book. The words are, *ut Parthos signa repetamus. Repeteremus* would seem more natural, but the great majority of editors refuse to alter the MS. reading from the present to the past tense. Crassus lost the standards in the year B.C. 53; they were restored to Augustus in B.C. 20. The use of the present tense implies an existing state of war, and suggests the expedition of L. Aurelius Verus against the Parthians during the years 162 to 165. The old and well-known phrase, "recovering standards," seems to be applied to the new war.

NOTE 3, page 14, line 26.
The reading of Baehrens has been followed.

NOTE 4, page 15, line 13.

As many of the early Christians in Rome were Jews, they inherited, so to speak, the prejudices with which the Jewish race was regarded by other nations. Whatever seemed ridiculous or odious in a Jew was imputed also to the Christian. It will be enough to say that the charges brought forward by Caecilius were due to the public ignorance both of Judaism and of Christianity.

Tacitus, giving a general account of the Jews in the fifth book of his History, says that in the course of their sojourn in the wilderness a troop of wild asses led them to a spring of water. He adds: "In their holy place they have consecrated an image of the animal by whose guidance they found deliverance from their long and thirsty wanderings."

There has been discovered at Rome, rudely scratched upon an ancient wall, the figure of a crucified man with the head of an ass. Another figure stands by as if in prayer, and underneath is a scrawl, "Alexamenos is worshipping God."

It may be noted that even in these days the ritual murder of children is occasionally alleged against the Jews by their ignorant enemies in parts of south-eastern Europe. Tacitus at least does them the justice to state that "it is a crime among them to kill any new-born infant."

Note 5, page 15, line 17.

In this sentence, only the purport of the Latin is indicated.

Note 6, page 16, line 13.

The references to Fronto of Cirta suggest that he was alive at the time of the dialogue. He lived from about 100 to 170.

Note 7, page 16, line 18.

In the Latin, instead of the words that ask this question, a description of the scene is given.

Note 8, page 17, line 18.

The reading of Baehrens is here followed.

Note 9, page 20, line 7.

The reading of Baehrens is here followed.

Note 10, page 23, line 21.

This seems to be the sense of a sentence which, if literally translated, would convey no meaning to an English reader. The Latin is: "*ecquid ad haec*" ait "*audet Octavius, homo Plautinae prosapiae, ut pistorum praecipuus, ita postremus philosophorum?*" "What reply can Octavius venture to make; a scion of the old Plautine stock, like his forbear, the first of bakers, but certainly the worst of philosophers?" The words *homo Plautinae prosapiae* indicate a quarrelsome or aggressive person; for Caecilius has not forgotten the disparaging remark of Octavius which provoked the dispute. Plautus, in the poverty of his younger days, had been a *pistor*. Perhaps a sneer is intended at journeymen and small tradesmen, and the classes from whom the Christians at that time were mainly recruited. The manuscript has *pistorum*, but, as this reading is not free from difficulty, various other words have been suggested by editors who have thought the manuscript patient of almost any emendation. *Christianorum*, from the contracted form *XPianorum*; *juris consultorum*, from the contraction *ICtorum*; and *disertorum*, from *dis'torum*, have been conjectured. Either of these would help the translator, but the fact that Plautus was a *pistor* is a cogent, if not an overpowering argument for the manuscript reading.

NOTE 11, page 27, line 22.
The reading of Baehrens has been followed.

NOTE 12, page 40, line 15.
It is strange that so cultivated a man as Minucius should accept the shallow rationalism of Euhemerus as accounting sufficiently for the pagan deities. Paganism, as he saw it, was far advanced in its decadence, and deserved his contempt; but he can hardly have failed to recognize in its origin something more than an easily explained imposture.

Note 13, page 44, line 8.
The translation omits the succeeding sentence.

Note 14, page 45, line 2.
The reading of Baehrens has been followed.

Note 15, page 47, line 3.
This passage on idols is closely paralleled by Clemens Alexandrinus in his Protrepticon, an appeal to the Greeks written at the end of the second century. He says: "Your idols must rank below the lowest animals. . . . Many animals cannot see, or hear, or make a sound; molluscs, for instance, cannot; but they live and grow, and are affected by the changes of the moon, while images do nothing at all, but are simply passive under the rough hand of the workman and the processes of manufacture. . . . Birds, again, such as swallows, and others, come in flocks and befoul the images without the slightest reverence for Olympian Jove, Aesculapius of Epidaurus, Minerva Polias, or Egyptian Serapis. . . . Parian marble is beautiful, but it is not yet Neptune. Ivory is beautiful, but it is not yet Jupiter. Matter always needs the help of art, while God needs nothing. Apply art to matter, and it receives form. It may be intrinsically valuable, but it is its form that renders it an object of veneration. It comes to this, then, that your statue is gold or wood, or stone—earth, in fact, if you regard

its ultimate origin—which has derived its form from the workman."

NOTE 16, page 49, line 4.
In this sentence the Latin is paraphrased.

NOTE 17, page 51, line 23.
In this, and in the preceding sentence only the purport of the Latin is indicated.

NOTE 18, page 53, line 21.
This is one of the passages on which Gibbon, in his fifteenth chapter, bases his remarks on the daemons. To that chapter we may refer the reader, reminding him, however, of Guizot's pertinent observation that "Gibbon has too often allowed himself to consider the peculiar notions of certain Fathers of the Church as inherent in Christianity."

The Magi were the priests of the Medes and Persians; but in the Acts of the Apostles, and here, the word is used in a secondary sense for those who practised occult or magical arts, perhaps combining sleight-of-hand with the wonders of elementary natural science.

NOTE 19, page 59, line 14.
This represents the purport of three sentences that are unfit for translation.

NOTE 20, page 60, line 27.

Trophies were usually made by setting up the arms and armour of the vanquished on a short pole or stump. In this way, the semblance of a human figure was, of course, produced.

NOTE 21, page 63, line 10.

This represents the purport of five sentences that are not translated.

NOTE 22, page 64, line 6.

In his fifteenth chapter Gibbon gives an estimate of the number of the Christians in Rome about fifty years later than the time of Minucius. He says: "The Church of Rome was undoubtedly the first and most populous of the empire; and we are possessed of an authentic record which attests the state of religion in that city about the middle of the third century, and after a peace of thirty-eight years. The clergy, at that time, consisted of a bishop, forty-six presbyters, seven deacons, as many sub-deacons, forty-two acolytes, and fifty readers, exorcists, and porters. The number of widows, of the infirm, and of the poor, who were maintained by the oblations of the faithful, amounted to 1,500. From reason, as well as from the analogy of Antioch, we may venture to estimate the Christians of Rome at about 50,000. The populousness of that great capital cannot, perhaps, be exactly ascertained;

but the most modest calculation will not surely reduce it lower than a million of inhabitants, of whom the Christians might constitute at the most a twentieth part."

NOTE 23, page 68, line 23.

This appears to be the sense of a corrupt passage, as to the reading of which no two editors are agreed.

NOTE 24, page 71, line 22.

A lacuna occurs here, according to Baehrens. Grammatically, the words on either side of the lacuna may be read together as one complete sentence; but there is little or no logical connexion between them.

NOTE 25, page 75, line 27.

A corrupt sentence, tentatively and conjecturally emended by many editors. The English is but a paraphrase of its apparent meaning.

NOTE 26, page 76, line 25.

This clause of the sentence paraphrases two clauses that are unfit for translation.

NOTE 27, page 78, line 18.

The reading of Baehrens has been followed.

CHISWICK PRESS: CHARLES WHITTINGHAM AND CO.
TOOKS COURT, CHANCERY LANE, LONDON.

Translations from Latin and Greek, uniform with this volume

Pott 8vo, 6s.
THE THOUGHTS OF MARCUS AURELIUS ANTONINUS. Translated literally, with Notes, Biographical Sketch, Introductory Essay on the Philosophy, and Index. By GEORGE LONG, M.A. Printed at the Chiswick Press on handmade paper, and bound in buckram.

2 vols. pott 8vo, 10s. 6d.
EPICTETUS. Arrian's Discourses, with the Encheiridion and Fragments. Translated, with Notes and Introduction, by GEORGE LONG, M.A. Printed at the Chiswick Press, on handmade paper, and bound in buckram.

This is the only complete English translation of Epictetus.

Pott 8vo, 4s. 6d.
ARISTOTLE ON THE ATHENIAN CONSTITUTION. Translated, with Introduction and Notes, by F. G. KENYON, M.A., Fellow of Magdalen College, Oxford. With an Autotype Facsimile of a portion of the original MS.

LONDON: GEORGE BELL & SONS
YORK STREET, COVENT GARDEN

CPSIA information can be obtained
at www.ICGtesting.com
Printed in the USA
BVHW042058281118
534029BV00042B/469/P